NEXTGEN LEARNERS PRESENTS

Think Like a Brain!™ Collection

The Brainy Bunch

Meet the Team Inside Your Head

BOOK 1

Think Like a Brain!™
Collection Overview

Think Like a Brain!™ is a wildly engaging, silly-smart children's book collection that invites kids to explore how their brains work from the inside out. Through playful characters, imaginative settings, and rhythm-rich storytelling, this collection teaches neuroscience, social-emotional learning (SEL), and self-understanding in ways children absorb without even realizing they are learning.

Instead of telling children how to behave or what to feel, Think Like a Brain!™ shows them why their brains respond the way they do. Each story transforms complex brain science into friendly characters and relatable moments, helping kids feel capable, curious, and empowered rather than confused or ashamed.

Designed for children first and embraced by parents and educators as preventative education, this collection supports:

- Emotional regulation and self-awareness
- Executive functioning skills
- Neurodivergent understanding and inclusion
- Brain-body connection and growth
- Compassion for self and others

With humor, heart, and factual accuracy at its core, Think Like a Brain!™ helps children build the skills many adults wish they had learned sooner, one playful page at a time.

One of the collection's most powerful features is how the characters become real-life reminders for children long after the story ends. Once kids learn who the characters are and what jobs they do, they can begin to recognize those same processes in themselves. A big feeling might become, "It looks like Amy is trying to tell you something," or a moment of pause might sound like, "What does your Fred think?" By naming experiences through familiar characters, children learn to notice what is happening inside their brains, reflect on it, and move forward more quickly with understanding rather than frustration.

Series 1:
The Brainy Bunch (Brain Anatomy)

Series Overview: Meet the brain's core parts as a friendly team. Kids learn what each part does and how they work together to help thinking, feeling, moving, and learning.

1. **The Brainy Bunch**
   Focus: Brain overview and teamwork
2. **Brainstem Benny and the Automatic Adventure**
   Focus: Breathing, heartbeat, survival basics
3. **Bella Cerebellum's Balance Ballet**
   Focus: Balance, coordination, practice
4. **Olly the Occipital Owl & The Lookout Tower**
   Focus: Vision, visual processing
5. **Tammy Temporal and the Soundy Sound Storm**
   Focus: Hearing, language, sound processing
6. **Perry the Parietal and the Body Map Bash**
   Focus: Touch, space, body awareness
7. **Hippocampus Hal and the Memory Maze**
   Focus: Memory, learning, recall
8. **Amy the Amygdala and the Overactive Alarm**
   Focus: Emotional alarm system, big feelings, pause before reacting
9. **Luna Lefty and Roger Righty's Mixed-Up Masterpiece**
   Focus: Left/right hemispheres, teamwork
10. **Callie the Connector and the Brain Bridge**
    Focus: Corpus callosum, brain-to-brain communication

Series 2:
Cortex Castle (Frontal Lobe Executive Functions)
Series Overview: A lively castle of executive-function helpers. Kids practice planning, starting, stopping, focusing, flexible thinking, time skills, and self-talk, with Frontal Fred guiding thoughtful choices.

1. **Cortex Castle**
   Focus: Executive function overview
2. **Frontal Fred and the Decision Dilemma**
   Focus: Decision-making, prioritizing
3. **Impulsive Ian and the Button Box**
   Focus: Impulse control, pause
4. **Memory Molly and the Wandering Thoughts**
   Focus: Working memory, holding steps
5. **Focus Frannie and the Great Distraction Chase**
   Focus: Attention, refocusing
6. **Planella and the Checklist Parade**
   Focus: Planning, sequencing
7. **Flexi and the Changey-Changeroo Day**
   Focus: Cognitive flexibility
8. **Self-Talk Sally and the Thoughtful Echoes**
   Focus: Self-talk, emotional regulation
9. **Starter Stacy & Finisher Finn**
   Focus: Task initiation, task completion
10. M**ilo the Minute Keeper & Mae the Moment Seeker**
   Focus: Time awareness, pacing
11. **The Power of Pausing with Penny**
   Focus: Pause skills, regulation

Series 3:
Busy Brain Café (Neurodivergent Affirmations)

Series Overview: A welcoming café where different brain styles are celebrated. These stories affirm neurodivergent experiences while teaching self-understanding, communication, and compassion for others.

1. **Nathan Neuron and the Bouncy Brain**
   Focus: ADHD metaphor, movement, attention
2. **Sara Sprinkle the Sensa and the Super Sensitive Day**
   Focus: Sensory sensitivity, overload tools
3. **Overwhelmed Owen and the Senses Overload**
   Focus: Sensory overload, coping strategies
4. **Interoceptive Ivy and the Inside Signals**
   Focus: Interoception, body signals
5. **Zane's Zigzag Thoughts and the Path to Peace**
   Focus: Anxiety, grounding
6. **The Busy Brain Café**
   Focus: Neurodivergent inclusion, different processing styles
7. **The Listening Light**
   Focus: Nonverbal communication, understanding
8. **The Language of Love**
   Focus: Connection, communication, compassion
9. **Trying Theo and the How-To Hiccup**
   Focus: Persistence, frustration tolerance
10. **Drowsy Drew and the Nighttime Repair**
    Focus: Sleep, brain repair
11. **Burned-Out Bonnie and the Rebuild**
    Focus: Burnout, rest, recovery

Series 4:
Steady Systems Squad (Regulation & Growth)

Series Overview: A squad that explains how brains regulate, reset, rest, and grow stronger over time, including stress waves, sleep crews, sensory filtering, and rebuilding after hard days.

1. **The Steady Systems Squad**
   Focus: Regulation systems overview
2. **Timothy Thalamus and the Traffic Tower**
   Focus: Sensory filtering, attention routing
3. **Danny Dimmer and Wake-Up Wonda**
   Focus: Arousal and alertness
4. **The Start, Stop, and Switch Station**
   Focus: Initiation, inhibition, shifting
5. **The Night Shift and the Sleepy Crew**
   Focus: Sleep systems, restoration
6. **The Stress Wave and the Return to Calm**
   Focus: Stress response, recovery
7. **The Brain Growth Gathering**
   Focus: Brain growth and development
8. **Paul's Practice Path**
   Focus: Neuroplasticity
9. **Daisy's Daydream Network**
   Focus: Daydream network, imagination
10. **Remy's Rebuild Crew**
    Focus: Recovery and healing

NEXTGEN LEARNERS PRESENTS

Think Like a Brain!™ Collection

The Brainy Bunch

Meet the Team Inside Your Head

BOOK 1

WRITTEN &
ILLUSTRATED BY:

MAISEL MCLAULA

NEXTGEN LEARNERS PRESS
CINCINNATI, OHIO

This book is published by NextGen Learners Press, an imprint of NextGen Learners LLC.

Maisel McLaula is a pen name used by the author of this work.

First Edition: 2026
Printed in the United States of America
ISBN: 978-1-972860-00-7

This book is intended for educational and informational purposes only. It is not intended to replace professional medical, psychological, or therapeutic advice, diagnosis, or treatment.
Always seek the advice of a qualified professional with any questions regarding a medical or mental health condition.

Artwork and visual elements in this book were created using a combination of original artwork, with enhanced original direction, digital illustration tools, and AI-assisted creative technologies.

A Note for My Readers:

Hi friend,
Your brain is incredible. It thinks, feels, remembers, solves, dances, creates, and so much more!
This series is here to help you understand how your brain works, and to cheer you on as you grow your own thinking superpowers.

Every part of your brain has a job.
Sometimes they get mixed up. That's okay!

When you learn what each part does, you can work with your brain instead of feeling like it's working against you.
So read, giggle, learn, and maybe even draw your own Brainy Bunch when you're done.

I'm cheering you on with every rhyme.

Think Like a Brain!™

Brain Anatomy Collection

Explore the castle inside your head! Meet each room and its brilliant resident, from Frontal Fred to Benny the Brainstem. Whimsy, wonder, and neurons await!

Dedicated to my amazing husband, Mickey McLaula. Through the way he accepted and loved me, I learned how everyone belongs in their own unique place. His love gave me courage, his support gave me space, and his belief in me made these books possible. He is the reason I continued this journey.

And to my students, you are why I created these characters. Your curiosity, challenges, laughter, and growth live inside every story.

And...

To the beautifully wired, the curiously wired, and the wonderfully neurodivergent minds.

You are exactly what a great brain looks like.

-Maisel McLaula

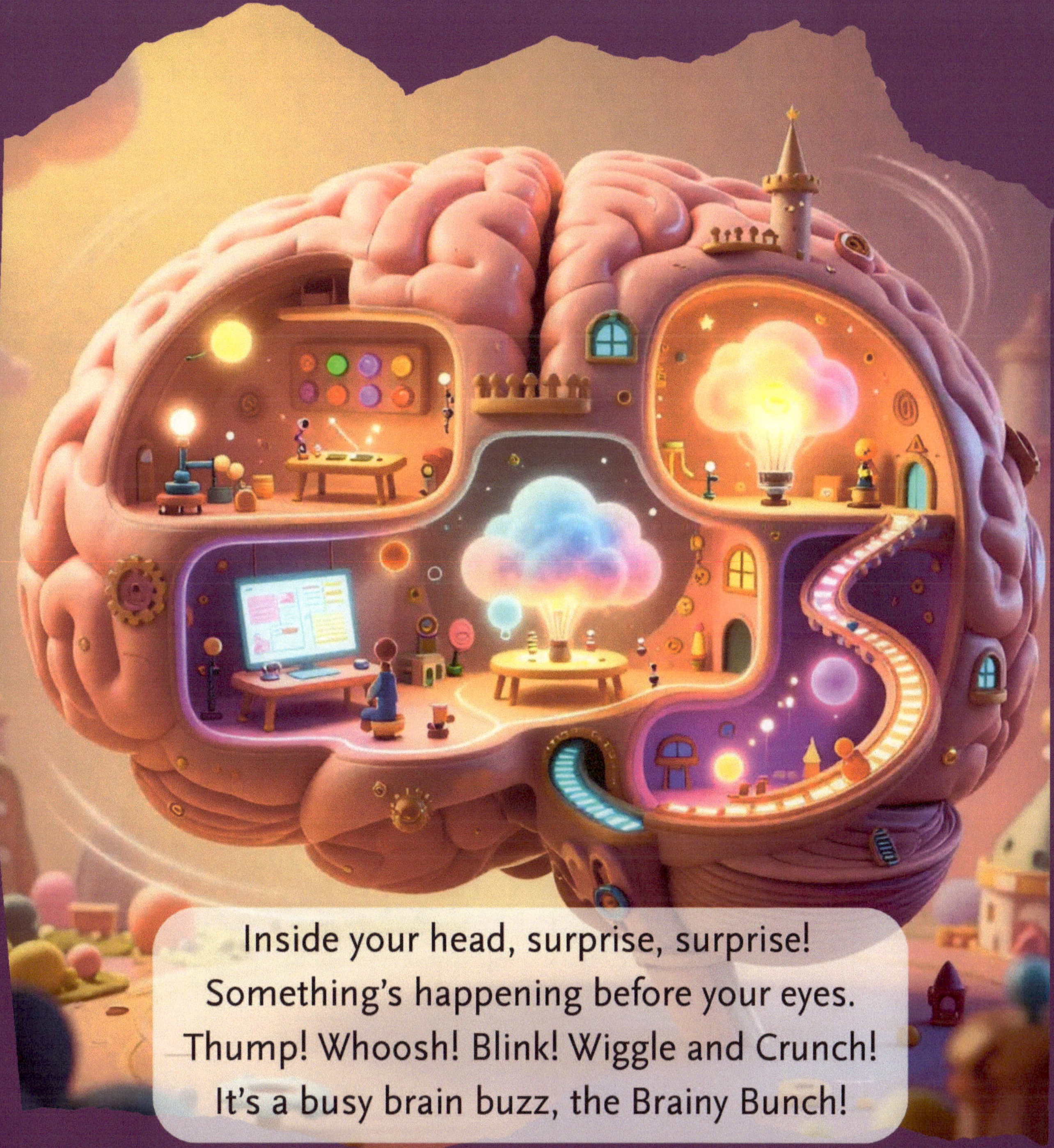

Inside your head, surprise, surprise!
Something's happening before your eyes.
Thump! Whoosh! Blink! Wiggle and Crunch!
It's a busy brain buzz, the Brainy Bunch!

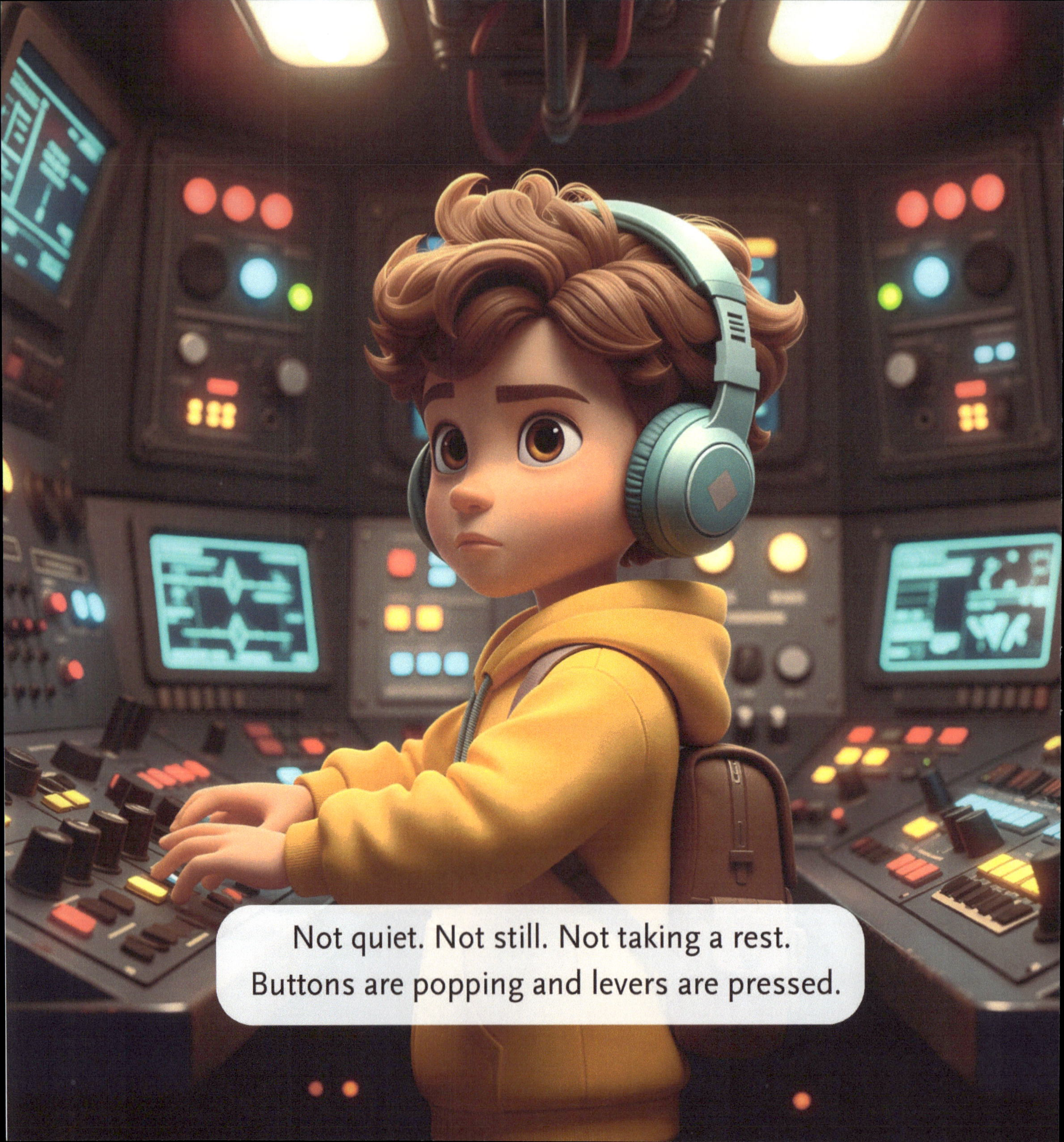

Not quiet. Not still. Not taking a rest.
Buttons are popping and levers are pressed.

Plans are zooming! Feelings go BOOM!
Ideas ping-pong from room to room.

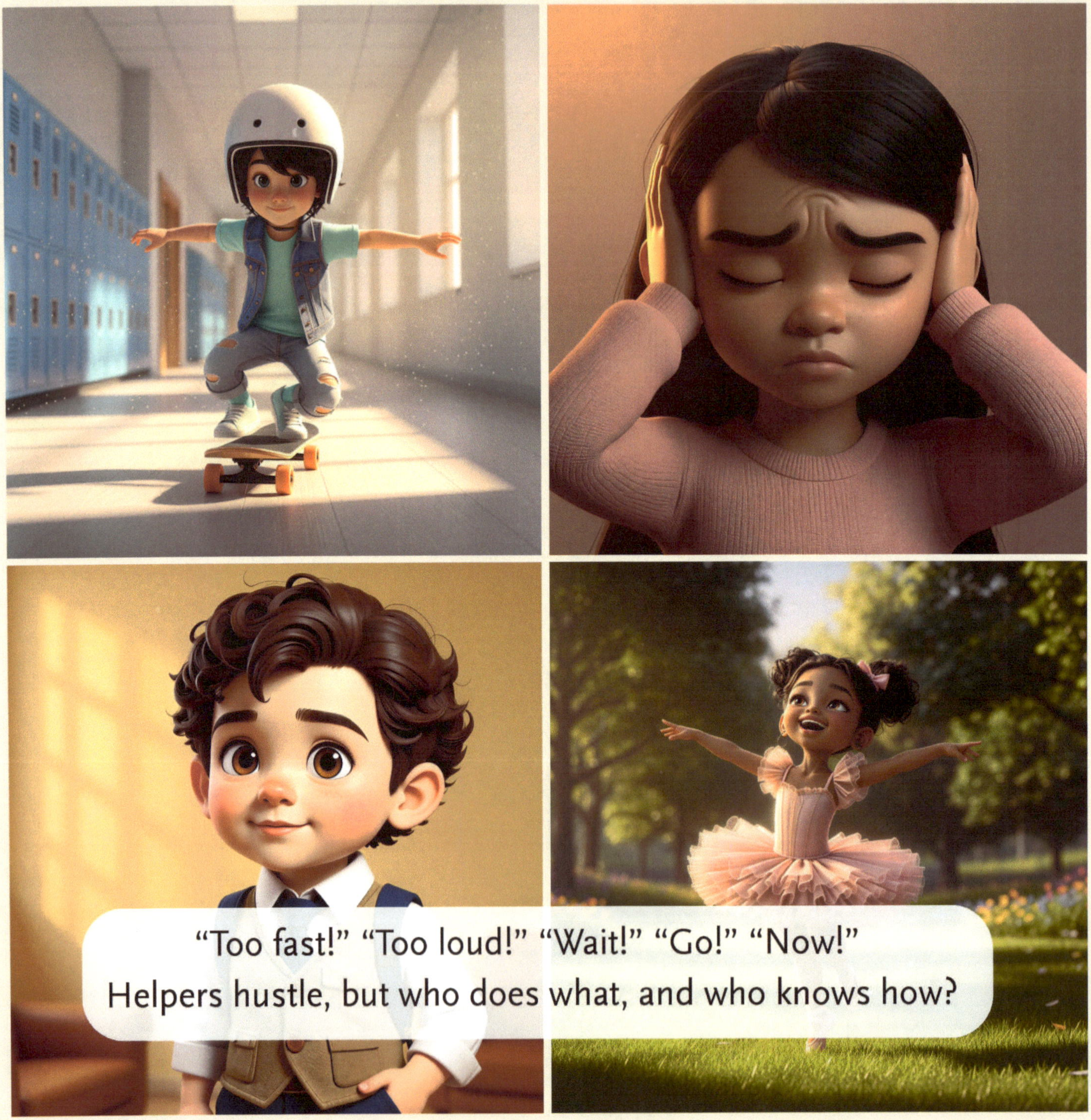

"Too fast!" "Too loud!" "Wait!" "Go!" "Now!"
Helpers hustle, but who does what, and who knows how?

Before their stories unfold one by one,
They popped in to greet you, just for fun.

Way down low, where it's steady and deep,
Where you breathe when you're awake or asleep,

Lives Benny the Brainstem, calm and small,
The busiest helper you'll never call.

He doesn't ask questions or wait for a cue,
He just keeps your body doing what bodies do.

Heartbeat. Breathing. Waking. Rest.
Benny keeps balance, he handles the rest.

Just above Benny, spinning just right,
Is Bella Cerebellum, graceful and bright.

She practices timing, balance, and flow,
Helping your body learn how to go.

When movements feel clumsy or wobbly one day,
Bella says, “Practice will smooth it this way.”

She learns with your body again and again,
Making motions feel easier, where? Right within.

At the very back, with eyes open wide,
Olly Occipital lives inside.

She gathers the light, the shapes, and the sight,
Turning what you see into pictures just right.

Flashy or bright? Too busy? Too new?
Olly asks for pauses to sort it all through.

She helps make seeing feel calmer and clear,
So pictures make sense instead of a blur.

Along the sides where echoes play,
Lives Tammy Temporal, listening all day.

She hears soft whispers and booms and song,
Helping sounds turn into words where it belongs.

When noise piles up and crashes like rain,
Tammy works best when rhythms stay sane.

Quiet and pattern help her do her best,
So sounds make sense, not a jumbled mess.

Right through the center, careful and aware,
Is Perry the Parietal, mapping you there.

He knows where your elbows, knees, and toes go,
Even with eyes closed, he still seems to know.

When bodies grow fast or space feels off-track,
Perry redraws the body's map.

With movement and touch and noticing too,
He helps your body feel safely you.

In twisty paths that twirl and bend,
Lives Hippocampus Hal, your memory friend.

He keeps your stories, the where and the when,
So you can remember them again and again.

When stress runs high or thoughts rush by,
Hal's paths may tangle, but he still tries.

With calm and cues and practice, too,
Lost memories wander back into view.

Up high and quick, with alarms on call,
Is Amy the Amygdala, watching it all.

She spots danger fast and feelings strong,
Shouting "Be careful!" when things feel wrong.

But Amy is learning, not every scare
Means danger is truly waiting there.

With help from her friends, she checks and slows,
So feelings can guide, not fully control.

Inside one brain, split left and right,
Live Luna and Roger, who sometimes fight.

One plans and orders steps neat and clear,
The other imagines with courage and creative cheer.

Different thinkers, both just right,
They work best together, side by side.

When they share ideas and listen too,
Big bright thinking comes shining through.

Holding it all, connecting each side,
Is Callie the Connector, steady and wide.

She sends thoughts back and forth with care,
So no good idea gets stuck over there.

When signals flow smoothly, side to side,
Thinking feels calmer deep inside.

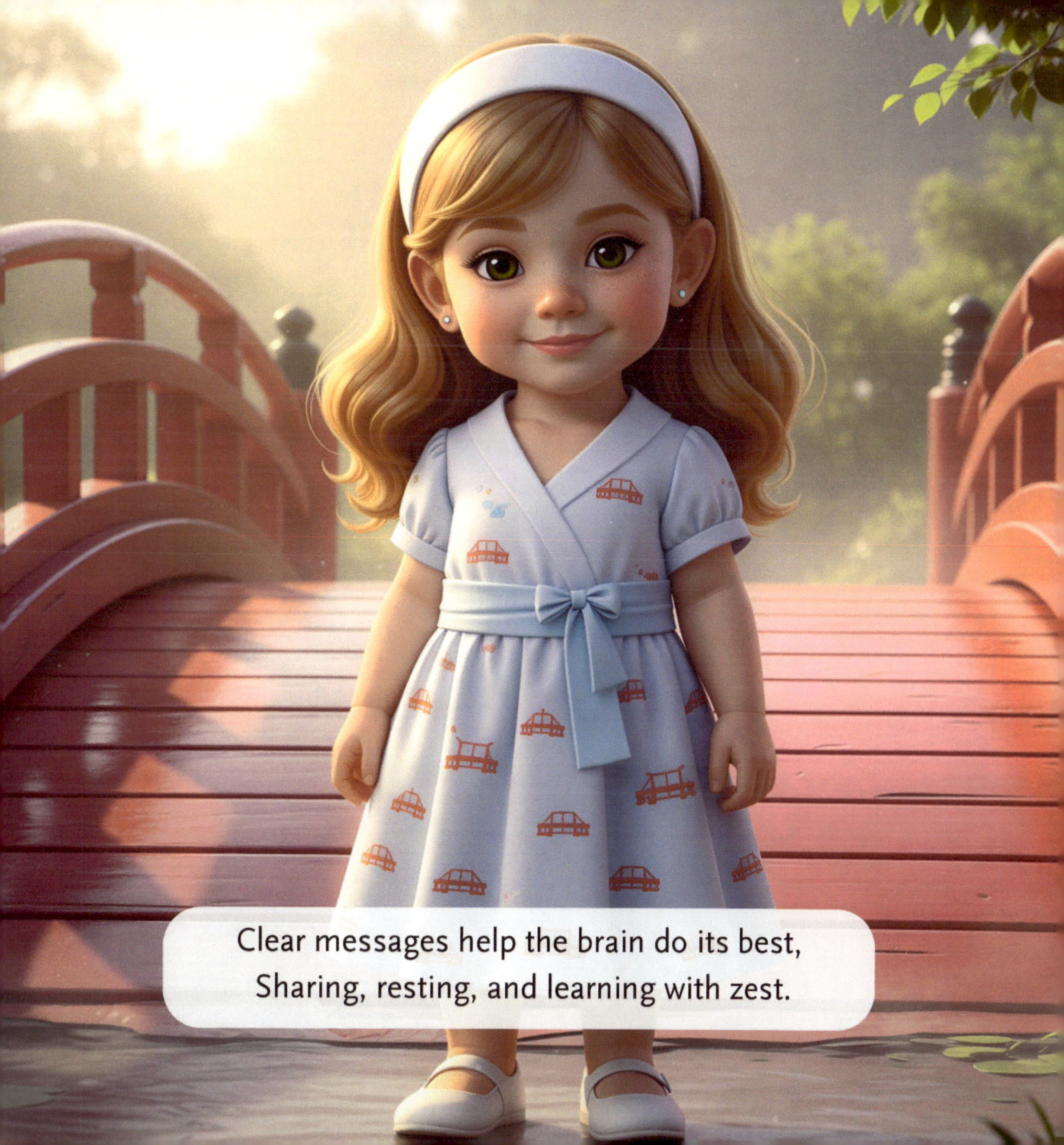
Clear messages help the brain do its best,
Sharing, resting, and learning with zest.

They don’t all agree. They don’t all lead.
But each plays a part your brain truly needs.

Some days feel easy. Some days feel tough.
Teamwork helps when things feel rough.

So when learning feels tricky or feelings feel new,
Remember the team that lives inside of you.

This book was their hello, your friendly first bunch.
Next, you'll meet them... one by one.

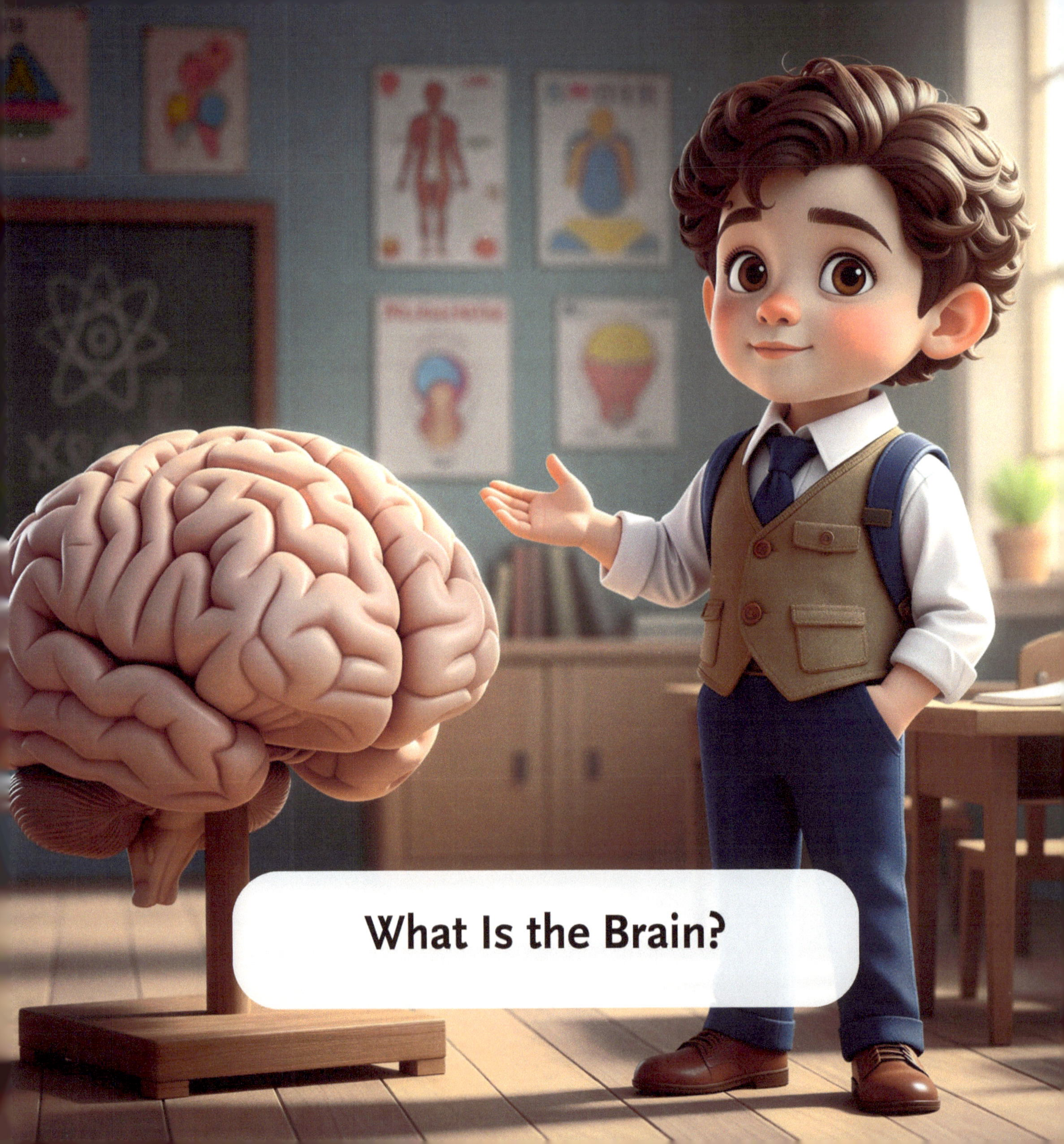

What Is the Brain?

Your brain is the boss of your body. It helps you think, learn, feel, move, remember, and make choices.

It tells your heart when to beat, your lungs when to breathe, and your muscles when to move.

Your brain also helps you understand the world, solve problems, and take care of yourself.

Every brain is different, and every brain is special.

Thank You to My Readers

Thank you for reading this book.
Whether you're a parent, a teacher,
a therapist, or a brilliant young
brain explorer,
your interest in understanding
how the mind works
means the world.

Sharing these books
means spreading compassion and
curiosity.

You are the reason
these stories come alive.
Thank you for believing in the
power of playful learning.

Stay curious. Stay kind.
Stay brainy!

The Brainy Bunch *Teacher & Parent Guide*

💡 What This Story Teaches:

- Core idea: The brain works as a team, not a single boss.
- Big message: Different brain parts help in different ways, and every part matters.
- Skills supported across this series: body regulation, balance and movement, sensory processing, memory and learning, emotional awareness, thinking styles, and brain-to-brain communication.
- Series philosophy: Children can learn how their brains work, not just what they feel.

This opening book introduces the whole Brainy Bunch so children (and grown-ups) understand that learning, behavior, and emotions come from many helpers working together.

Key Concepts for Grown-Ups

Each Brainy Bunch character represents a real brain region. This first story is an orientation, not a lesson on mastery. Later books zoom in on one character at a time.

Important foundations:

- Regulation comes before learning.
- Big behaviors usually signal overwhelmed systems.
- Skills develop through experience, not pressure.
- Understanding replaces shame.

Children do not need to read these books in order. Think of the series as a flexible toolbox. You can choose stories based on what a child needs most right now.

Examples:

- Dysregulated or tired → Benny
- Wobbly or uncoordinated → Bella
- Visually overwhelmed → Olly
- Sound sensitive → Tammy
- Clumsy or growing fast → Perry
- Forgetful or learning new material → Hal
- Big emotions or anxiety → Amy
- Creative vs logical tension → Luna & Roger
- Trouble integrating ideas → Callie

This empowers adults to respond to needs rather than labels.

Meet the Brainy Bunch

- **Benny the Brainstem** – body safety, breathing, calm, balance, sleep-wake cycles
- **Bella Cerebellum** – coordination, rhythm, timing, practice, motor learning
- **Olly Occipital** – vision, visual processing, filtering visual input
- **Tammy Temporal** – sound, language, rhythm, auditory understanding
- **Perry Parietal** – body awareness, touch, spatial sense, mapping the body
- **Hippocampus Hal** – memory formation, learning, recall, organizing experiences
- **Amy Amygdala** – emotional alarms, safety signals, fear and protection
- **Luna Lefty & Roger Righty** – thinking styles: logic, language, creativity, imagination
- **Callie the Connector** – communication between brain hemispheres

Each helper contributes something essential. No single character runs the whole brain.

🗣️ Discussion Starters

- Which Brainy Bunch character feels most like you today?
- Who do you think helps you most at school or at home?
- Who would you like to learn more about next?
- Do different days need different helpers?
- Can you notice when your body, feelings, or thoughts need support?

Encourage children to share without correcting their answers. Curiosity builds awareness.

Try This Together:

1. Draw Your Brain Team

Invite children to draw the Brainy Bunch and add their own helpers. Ask what each helper does.

2. Pick-a-Character

Let children choose which character they want to explore next based on how they feel.

3. Brain Check-In

Ask three simple questions:

- How does your body feel?
- How do your feelings feel?
- How do your thoughts feel?

4. Character Call-Outs

Use character names in daily life:

"That sounds like Amy."

"Let's call Benny."

"Bella needs practice."

🎯 Bonus Challenge

Create a Brainy Bunch Wall or Board.
Add each character as you read their story. Let children move characters closer when they need that helper.

Optional labels:

- Body Helpers
- Feeling Helpers
- Thinking Helpers

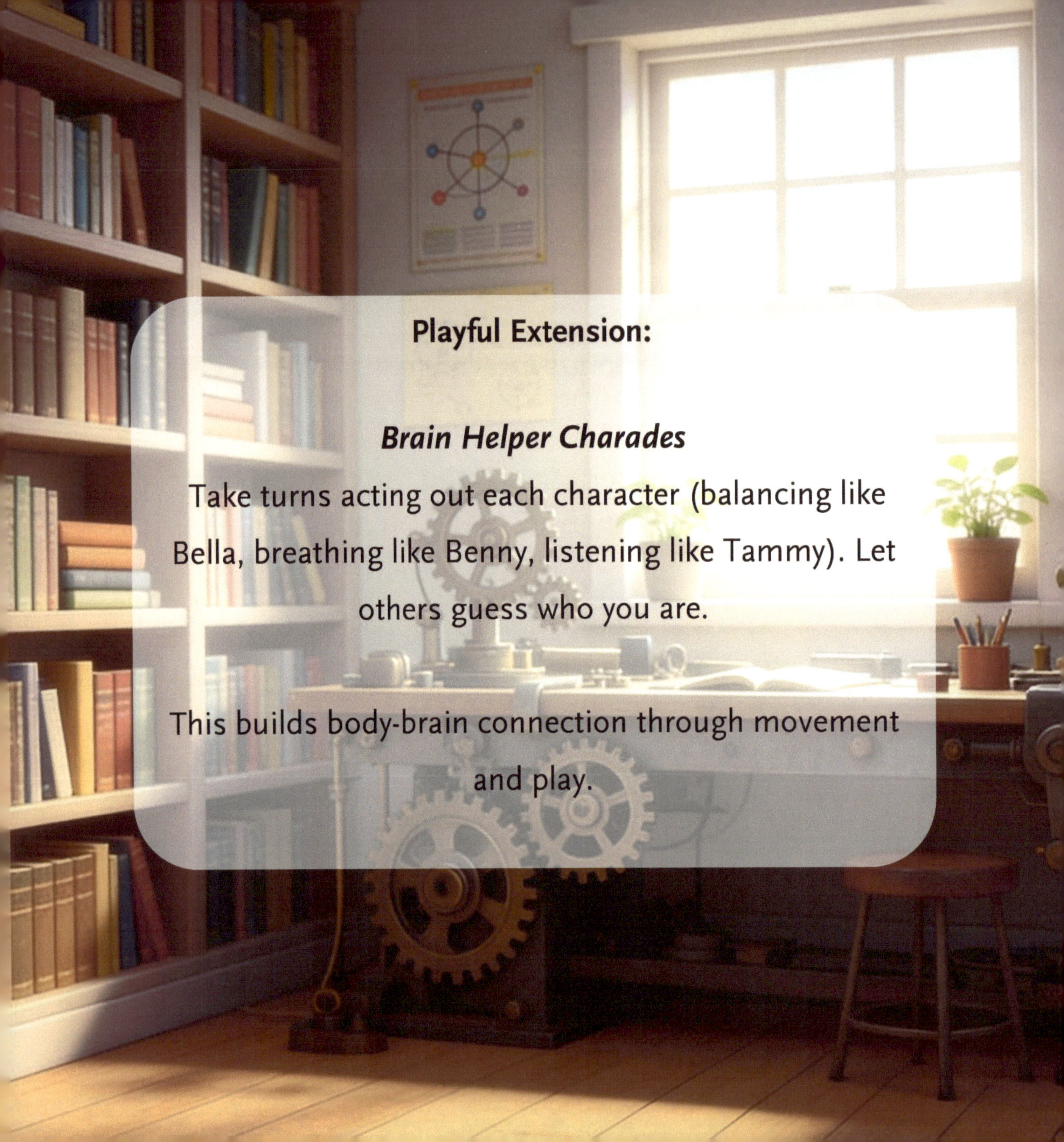

Playful Extension:

Brain Helper Charades

Take turns acting out each character (balancing like Bella, breathing like Benny, listening like Tammy). Let others guess who you are.

This builds body-brain connection through movement and play.

🛠️ The Brainy Bunch Toolbox:

Use these principles across the whole series:

- Follow the child's nervous system, not the lesson plan.
- Re-read favorite characters often.
- Pair stories with movement whenever possible.
- Normalize struggle as part of learning.
- Externalize skills using character language.
- Offer regulation before correction.
- Keep tools simple and repeatable.

Helpful phrases:

- "Let's help your body first."
- "Which helper do you need right now?"
- "Your brain is learning."

❤️ Final Note for Grown-Ups

The Brainy Bunch exists to help children understand themselves, not to fix them.

When kids learn that their brains are teams, they gain language for their experiences, compassion for their struggles, and confidence in their growth.

Calm, focus, memory, and emotions are not traits children should already have. They are skills children learn, with patient support.

This series is meant to grow alongside them.

Resources & GROWTH

Resources:

(Overview of major brain parts and how they work together)

- NINDS (NIH). Brain Basics: Know Your Brain / Brain Basics resources. (2024–2025).
- Cleveland Clinic. Brain: parts and function (overview pages). (2025 update).
- CASEL. CASEL's SEL Framework (self-awareness, self-management, social awareness, relationship skills, responsible decision-making). (2020, updated).
- CDC. Child Development: Positive Parenting Tips and developmental guidance by age. (2024–2025).
- MedlinePlus (U.S. National Library of Medicine)
- Encyclopedia Britannica

Growth:

(If you or someone you know wants to strengthen calming, body regulation, or back-to-steady routines)

- Harvard Center on the Developing Child
  - Look for: brain architecture, how the brain develops
- American Academy of Pediatrics (HealthyChildren.org)
  - Search: brain development in children

Acknowledgments:

To my students: past, present, and future:
You taught me more than any textbook ever could. By watching how you explored, questioned, struggled, and discovered, I learned how minds truly grow. Every "aha" moment in these pages began with you.

To the parents, teachers, and guides walking beside children every day:
Thank you for listening, for advocating when things feel complicated, and for believing that understanding a child's inner world truly matters. Your patience and care shape futures in ways you may never fully see.

To my husband, my best friend, and my constant partner in learning:
Thank you for walking beside me, believing in this work, and holding space for creativity to exist. Sharing curiosity, growth, and creation with you has been one of the greatest honors of my life.

To the great thinkers who shaped how I see the world: including Dr. Seuss, Albert Einstein, Leonardo da Vinci, Stephen Hawking, Ludwig van Beethoven, just to name a few, and my English teacher, Mrs. Godfrey:
Your curiosity, courage, and imagination reminded me that learning is limitless, creativity is powerful, and questions matter. Mrs. Godfrey, your encouragement, belief in me, and love of words sparked my writing journey. If not for you, I may never have picked up a pen.

And to my publisher, NextGen Learners™
It was by fate that we met, and by inspiration that we now move forward. Together, we build something meaningful. Together, we leave this legacy.

Lastly, to my own brain:
Complex, resilient, ever-adapting, and endlessly learning. Thank you for carrying stories, holding wonder, and reminding me that growth is always possible.

Maisel McLaula is the author of the Think Like a Brain!™ children's book collection, a story-first series that blends neuroscience, imagination, and emotional safety for young readers.

Drawing from decades of experience supporting children and families, her work centers on a simple but powerful belief: children deserve to understand and accept who they are, including how their brains work and why they make the choices they do.

Through playful characters and gentle metaphors, Maisel's stories help children discover the "why" behind their thoughts, feelings, and actions, turning confusion into clarity and self-judgment into self-compassion. By understanding their inner systems, children gain the power to respond with kindness toward themselves and to recognize those same patterns in others.

Maisel believes that when children feel safe inside their own minds, empathy grows naturally. The Think Like a Brain!™ collection offers a foundation for confidence, understanding, and care that grows with the child.

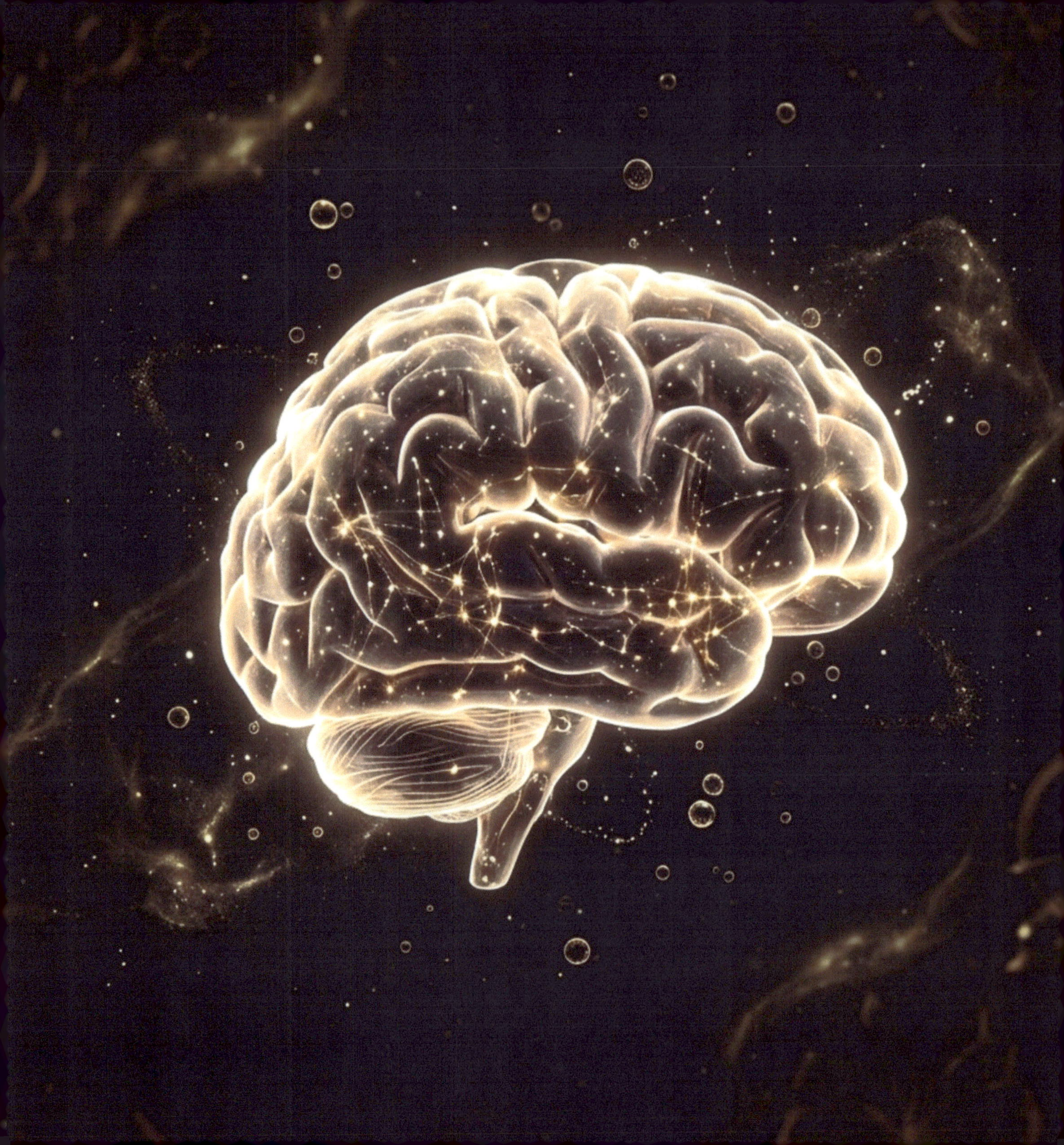

ABOUT THE PUBLISHER

NextGen Learners LLC is an educational publishing company dedicated to helping children understand how they think, feel, learn, and grow.

Through imaginative storytelling, neuroscience-informed concepts, and real-world application, NextGen Learners creates books and resources that support emotional development, critical thinking, self-awareness, and confidence in young minds.

Our work is designed not only for children, but for the parents, educators, caregivers, and professionals who walk beside them. Each book serves as a bridge, helping adults better understand the child in front of them, while helping children better understand themselves.

By creating shared language and meaningful connection points, our stories foster deeper relationships, reduce misunderstanding, and encourage acceptance, both within oneself and toward others.

We believe every child's mind is uniquely wired, and that understanding those differences is the foundation for compassion, growth, and lifelong learning.
With multiple collections designed to support cognitive, emotional, and developmental growth, NextGen Learners provides tools that children can carry with them, and tools that adults can use to guide them with clarity, patience, and purpose.

MORE TO EXPLORE

The Brainy Bunch is just the beginning.
More stories, tools, and brain-friendly resources are on the way! Designed to help children, parents, and educators better understand how the brain works in everyday life.

FREE PRINTABLES

We've created printable pages to go along with this book, including:

-Reading Guides

-Brain helper visuals

-Character Cards

These are available for free as part of our growing resource library.

Our full website experience is built to include:

--Downloadable activity packs

-Parent & teacher guides

-Expanded learning tools

-Additional collections and topics

STAY CONNECTED

We love hearing how children connect with these stories!

If there is a topic, feeling, or challenge you would like to see explored in future books, we would love to hear from you!

Contact us: Inspire@NextGenLearners.com
NextGenLearners.com

Your ideas help shape future stories and support the growth of this collection.

This collection grows with you. New resources and stories are added regularly.

Maisel McLaula loves hearing from the tiny humans who read her books.

Did a story make you giggle, spark a big idea, or inspire you to draw your very own character? She would be delighted to see it! Send your letters and artwork to:

NextGen Learners
Attn: Maisel McLaula
8666 Beechmont Ave #1063
Cincinnati, OH 45255

Every letter is read with a smile, and your artwork just might make her whole day.

OPEN BRAIN

www.ingramcontent.com/pod-product-compliance
Lightning Source LLC
Chambersburg PA
CBHW041321210926
51847CB00002B/17
9781972860007